101 FUN & Petty WAYS to ANNOY YOUR CAT

Text by Jim Erskine
Illustrations by Jess Erskine

Rolling Donut Press

101 Fun & Petty Ways
to Annoy Your Cat

Published by Rolling Donut Press

www.RollingDonutPress.com

Yes, we love our kitty cats.
But:

As every cat owner knows, a cat's #1 purpose in life is to annoy you. So they really do deserve whatever payback you can come up with from time to time. This little book exists just to show you there's always a creative and satisfying way to respond to their brand of crap.

Some of these annoyances are just simple, mindless fun. Some are totally ridiculous activities that can potentially embarrass both you and your cat thoroughly. And others are merely daydreams and wishful thinking. But on those days when it seems your cat is practically begging for a response to all the attitude they dish out, we suspect they'll **all** look pretty good to you.

(And just so nobody flips out about this book: We do not condone the physical abuse of any animal whatsoever. This is a humor book, not a "how to" guide.)

If you are inspired to attempt a little juvenile kitty cat revenge, just keep in mind how much silliness your furry feline is willing to take from you before the cat poop hits the fan. And be sure to make up after play time is done.

Happy annoying!

- Jim Erskine & Jess Erskine

Help your cat draw a picture of you.

Hypnotize your cat.

Yodel.

Perform a tap dance for your cat's enjoyment.

Open up other cans of food (soup, vegetables, etc.) in the kitchen when it's close to feeding time.

Chirp and tweet like a bird.

Share a pickle with your cat.

Spy on them.

Play "blubba blubba blubba"
with your cat's lips.

Have a staring contest.

Play together for one minute
just to get your cat wound up,
then stop and go do something else.

Trace your cat's paws.

Stretch your cat out in a "super kitty" pose,
then run around house making them fly.

Paint your cat's nails.

Turn the stereo on full blast
when your cat is sleeping on it.

Count your cat's whiskers.

Stop what you're doing and stare at your cat while they groom themselves.

Give a running commentary of their actions: *"Lick, lick, lickety, lick, lick, lick, lick, lick, lickety, lickety, lick, lick, lick, lick, lick... bite bite bitey bite bite... lick, lick, lickety, lick, lick..."*

When your cat stops grooming, muss up their fur again.

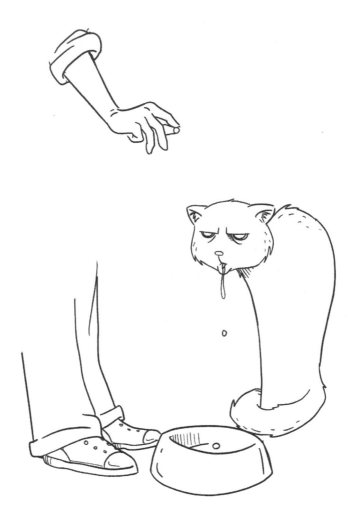

At feeding time, drop just One. Piece. of.
Food. in the cat's bowl at a time.

Spin your cat on the linoleum in the kitchen.

Pretend you are a dog.

Blow gently in your cat's face.

Drop your clothes on your cat whenever
they watch you undress.

Wrap a plastic grocery bag around their waist.

Smear a dab of cheese whiz
on your cat's haunches.

Give your cat a water balloon to play with.

Wash their butt with a wet wipe whenever it
smells like poop.

Put their hairballs in their food dish.

Place a mirror next to the litter box so your cat can have company.

Stomp.

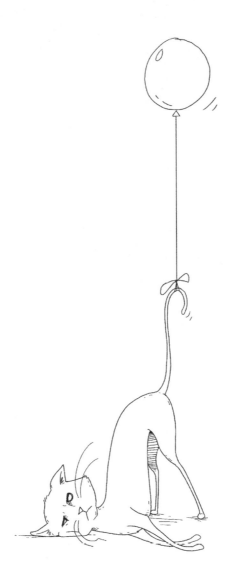

Tie a balloon to their tail.

When your cat yawns, grab their tongue.

Rub a clingy piece of cellophane on a sweater, then stick it on your cat.

See how long you can keep your cat's tail motionless.

Style their fur with hair gel.

When your cat isn't looking,
clap once, then pretend
you didn't do it.

Tie a string to their food bowl and
pull it slowly away when they try to eat.

Give your cat a collar with lots of
jingle bells.

Dress your cat in doll clothes.

Give your cat an incredibly embarrassing nickname.

Grab their paw, shake it, and say, "How do you do!" over and over.

Make your cat pose for a photo.

Smother your cat with kisses.

Never let your cat actually catch
their play toy.

When your cat meows at you,
meow back as obnoxiously as you can.

Talk to your cat face to face,
with your mouth full of food.

Make your cat wear a wig.

Hiss.

Play "It's Raining!" with your cat whenever you are washing the dishes.

Put your laundry basket over the food bowl.

Point at your cat from just an inch or so
away, and say "I'm not touching you"
over and over.

Very gently put your finger on their forehead, and hold it there.

Stick a small piece of tape on your cat's paw.

Pretend your cat is a ventriloquist's dummy.

Tie some yarn on their tail.

Make a Kitty Cat Shot Gun:
Hold your cat's front legs together in one
hand, back legs in other. Aim cat like
shotgun. Make appropriate shooting and
reloading noises.

Play tickle toes.

Dip their back paw in water.

Knit kitten mittens.

Laugh out loud heartily at random, unexpected moments.

Just as your cat is walking by, move your foot suddenly.

Lay some loose packing tape (sticky side up) on the floor in front of their food dish.

Turn your cat's ears inside out.

Baptize your cat.

Wake your cat up from their nap
by holding an empty cat food can
in front of their nose.

Brush your cat's teeth.

Put a sticker on your cat's forehead.

Attach hair clips to your cat's back.

Blow gently in their ear.

Rub their fur the wrong way.

"Shame" your cat.

"Accidentally" shut your cat in another room when it's time to eat.

Turn your head suddenly and stare at your cat.

Scream.

Put some food in the bottom of a styrofoam cup, so the cup will get stuck on your cat's head.

When your cat yawns, gently stick your finger in their mouth.

Teach your cat how to twerk.

Wrap Mardi Gras beads around their midsection.

Pick up your cat,
hold him close,
hum a song
and dance together.

Cover your cat's food bowl with plastic wrap.

Pretend your cat doesn't exist.

Take your cat for a bike ride.

Tear a hole in a piece of bread and put it
over your cat's head like a bonnet.

Hold your cat's back legs and walk it like a wheelbarrow.

Play peek-a-boo.

Stand with your feet on either side of them.

Swaddle your cat.

Play "I'm poking you on this side! Now I'm poking you on this side! Now I'm poking you on this side again!"

Use your cat as a pillow.

Whenever there's any cause for a celebration, make your cat wear a huge party hat.

Play "squishy kitty face".

Teach your cat to sign his own name.

When your cat is curled up and relaxed in your lap, pick him up under his arms and start his exercise and stretching routine. One – two, one - two.

Put a can of cat food on their dish, upside down.

Gently set small objects on top of your cat
while they are sleeping.

Massage their head.

Make up a super annoying theme song for your cat and sing it every time they come into the room.

Twiddle your cat's whiskers while they are sleeping.

Give your cat attention only when
it isn't wanted.

Make your cat wear a diaper.

Get a barking dog ringtone.

Build a pillow fort around your cat.

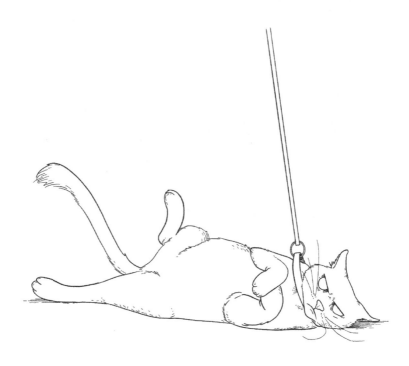

Walk your cat on a leash.

Measure your cat's tail.

Attach a ribbon to each leg.

Imitate every move your cat makes.

Ambush your cat with stuffed animals.

Make your cat participate in a stuffed animal parade.

Play dog videos on your TV.

Put panty hose on your cat's head.

Sit down with your cat and read your Last Will and Testament to them, making it clear that they will not inherit anything, so don't get any ideas.

Declare a truce,
embrace each other's faults,
and co-exist as best you can.

(At least until the NEXT time
they annoy you...)

Also from Rolling Donut Press:

Cooking With Cats: A Coloring Book

52 Simple Reasons Why I Love You

2 AM Angst: A Coloring Book for Sleepless Nights

Finish the Drawing, Volume I

Finish the Drawing, Volume II

Coupons for Couples

Said No Nurse Ever:
A Coloring Book for Nurses Who've Seen It All

Sh*t That Drives Me Crazy

Wow! Can We Do That Again?

50 Reasons Why I Love You, Mom

The Coloring Book Diet

Creative Minds Never Sleep

*Find them all on Amazon
& other online booksellers!*

Love you... bye!

Made in the USA
Monee, IL
23 February 2021